SHAW'S CORNER

Hertfordshire

The National Trust

Discovering Shaw's Corner

In 1904 George Bernard Shaw wrote to his friend H.G. Wells, 'We are in the agonies of house-hunting. Now is the time to produce an eligible residence if you have one handy.' Two years later the Shaws came to Ayot St Lawrence. They had already rented a house in nearby Welwyn, but finding it too large, continued looking for somewhere easily accessible from London, yet providing peace and quiet for Shaw to write. In Ayot St Lawrence he discovered a tombstone dedicated to 'Mary Anne South. Born 1825. Died 1895. Her time was short.' Shaw felt that if 70 was considered young for people living in the village, then this was the place for him to settle so that he could devote many years to his writings. He was not deceived; he died in November 1950 aged 94, mentally and physically active to the last.

Neither of the Shaws liked their new home, something which suited them well, as it did not distract from Charlotte's love of travelling or Shaw's passion for work. Renting the house until 1920, the Shaws then bought it from the Church for £6,220. Although originally called the New Rectory, the villagers started calling the house 'Shaw's Corner' after Shaw had overcome their initial misgivings at his reputation for being both eccentric and a socialist. Edith Reeves, a neighbour, commented that 'the villagers all thought he was a rum one, a very rum one... and it was not until 1915, during the terrible Hertfordshire blizzard, that the village in general got to know him more closely. He came out and worked hard with the other menfolk for days on end, sawing up trees which had been torn up by their roots and lay blocking the road.'

Although Shaw moved to the village to hide away from people, he intended his home to become a literary shrine, a place of pilgrimage for his many admirers. This contradiction in his life – between publicity-seeking self-promotion and a need for peace and quiet – reveals the division in Shaw's character. 'GBS' was the public face of the private 'Bernard Shaw'.

I have advertised myself so well that I find myself, whilst still in middle life, almost as legendary a person as the Flying Dutchman.

Preface for *Three Plays for Puritans* (1901)

The Tour of the House begins on p.19.

'The Chucker Out' of outmoded Victorian convention: GBS on the veranda in July 1950

Shaw wrote prolifically from the 1880s until his death in 1950. 'If a man is a deep writer all his works are confessions' (*Shaw Gives Himself Away*, 1939)

Facing south, 'The Riviera' was the ideal place to sit in the sunshine and entertain guests

Shaw's parents, George and Lucinda Carr Shaw.
'The best brought up children are those who have
seen their parents as they are. Hypocrisy is not the
parents' first duty' (*Maxims for Revolutionists*).
'Parentage is a very important profession, but no
test of fitness for it is ever imposed in the interest
of the children' (*Everybody's Political What's What*)

33 Synge Street, Dublin –
Shaw's birthplace.
This photograph sits on
the mantelpiece in the
Dining Room

Childhood in Ireland

George Bernard Shaw was born in a small house in Synge Street in Dublin on 26 July 1856, the third child and only son of George and Lucinda Shaw. He later described his Protestant family as impoverished aristocrats and 'snobs to the backbone', and his childhood as 'rich only in dreams, frightful and loveless in realities'. His parents' marriage was strained: his father was professionally unsuccessful and an alcoholic, his mother absorbed in local musical productions and the musician George Vandeleur Lee. The resulting ménage-à-trois affected Shaw's views on his own relationships, leading to emotional self-denial and a feeling of rejection. Uncertain about the true identity of his father, he loathed the name George, always preferring to be called Bernard, and the twin themes of blood relationships and illegitimacy recur constantly in his plays. As a child, his home life was unhappy, and his school days disappointing. His only solace and hope of self-education was visiting the National Gallery of Ireland.

At the age of 20 Bernard Shaw followed his mother and Vandeleur Lee to London. Although he was to spend the rest of his life based in England, his early Irish experiences greatly influenced his character and approach to life, and he never lost his strong Irish brogue. Shaw's first shocking encounter with Dublin's slums as a rent collector for the land agents, Uniacke Townshend & Co., was later recalled in his first play, *Widowers' Houses* (1892). Summer holidays spent at Torca Cottage on Dalkey Hill near Dublin gave the young Shaw a sense of beauty and joy that he never forgot, and perhaps never felt again. Once in London, Shaw turned to the realities of life by becoming a socialist.

Torca Cottage, Dalkey Hill, where Shaw became 'a prince in a world of my own imagination'

The view from Torca. 'I owe more than I can express to the natural beauty of that enchanting situation commanding the two great bays between Howth and Bray Head'

5

Early Life in London, 1876–92

The Reading Room of the British Museum about 1876: 'My debt to that great institution is inestimable'

'William Morris was great not only among little men but among great ones'

Sidney Webb, a leading figure in the Fabian Society and great friend and mentor of Shaw

Having arrived in London, Shaw embarked on a vigorous programme of self-education, visiting the National Gallery on its free days, spending much of his time in the Reading Room of the British Museum, reading volumes on polite behaviour to overcome his shyness, and practising his public-speaking techniques. He came under the influence of early socialist movements, including the Fellowship of New Life (founded in 1882), whose ideals of individual improvement through manual work, woollen clothes and vegetarianism had a lasting effect. He also joined the Fabian Society (founded in 1884), which put social improvement before individual improvement, believing that if progress was left to individuals, the pace of change would be too slow. By contrast, William Morris's Socialist League, an alternative group formed at much the same time, favoured more revolutionary tactics.

The Fabian movement gave Shaw an overwhelming sense of public duty, as the leading Fabians were selfless and almost puritanical. Shaw spent much of his time at political meetings, but most of his extraordinary energy was poured into writing, at first into novels. It was through his fifth book – *The Unsocial Socialist* – that he came into contact with William Morris. Shaw became an enthusiastic protégé of Morris in his later years, admiring his 'artistic taste of great integrity' and calling him 'four great men rolled into one'.

Shaw's literary work and political beliefs overlapped from an early stage. However, from a financial viewpoint his early literary efforts were unsuccessful. Consequently, Shaw earned his living through journalism, first as an art critic for *The World* between 1886 and 1890, and later as a music critic for *The Star* under the pen name of 'Corno di Bassetto'.

(*Opposite*) GBS as a young man in London

Beginnings of being a Playwright

Shaw's admission card to the Reading Room of the British Museum

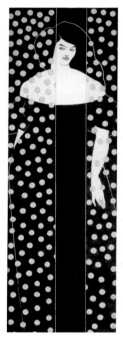

Aubrey Beardsley's design for a poster advertising *Arms and the Man* (1894)

'The ideal love affair is one conducted by post. My correspondence with Ellen Terry was a wholly satisfactory love affair ... she got tired of five husbands; but she never got tired of me'

While reading in the British Museum one day, Shaw's neighbour, William Archer, introduced himself, intrigued at the thought of someone simultaneously reading Marx's *Das Kapital* in French and the full orchestral score of Wagner's *Tristan and Isolde*. Archer was a leading drama critic, who became a close friend of Shaw and was instrumental in getting him his first work as a journalist in 1885. Their friendship also led to their collaboration on what was to become his first play, *Widowers' Houses*.

As far as Bernard Shaw was concerned, humour was a serious business. His plays became vehicles to forward the Fabian permeation of society, and beneath the wit, audacity and constant flood of aphorisms was an almost puritanical zeal to infuse society with his political beliefs. Common themes that run throughout Shaw's plays include capitalism, the role of women in society, the struggle for self-improvement, and rebellion against accepted beliefs and conventions. He admitted that 'All Shaw's characters are himself: mere characters stuck up to spout Shaw'.

Shaw wrote no explicit biography; yet the people he met and the situations he faced often formed the basis for his works. Friends and colleagues turn into characters; conflicts reappear as plots; Shavian beliefs run through as themes. So the clear-headed, practical Fabian Sidney Webb appears as Bluntschli in *Arms and the Man* (1894), and his wife Beatrice Webb was combined with a well-known liberal feminist Mrs Orme to become Vivie in *Mrs Warren's Profession* (1898).

Music was also fundamental to Shaw's development as a playwright. He declared that no-one could understand him without being 'soaked in symphonies and operas ... far more completely than in literary drama'.

Through his work in the theatre, politics and the women's movement, Shaw came into contact with many leading actresses, Fabian benefactresses and early feminists, including Florence Farr, Ellen Terry, Annie Besant, E. Nesbit and Eleanor Marx. Many of them found Shaw charismatic and charming, and in return he found in them an opportunity to explore his emotions without commitment to marriage. He broke many hearts, notably that of William Morris's daughter, May.

The actress Florence Farr, who commissioned *Arms and the Man*: 'All her men friends fell in love with her'

Shaw rehearsing *Arms and the Man* at the Avenue Theatre, London, in 1894

9

Charlotte Payne-Townshend

The Shaws on honeymoon. 'She was a real helpmate and constant companion in all aspects of his life. Theirs was that sort of marriage' (Fred Drury, gardener at Shaw's Corner)

Charlotte with the house cat

Introduced to each other in January 1896, Charlotte Payne-Townshend and Bernard Shaw found they had much in common: both were born into Irish Protestant families within six months of each other and both had suffered from a 'perfectly hellish childhood and youth'.

In August that year Beatrice Webb noted in her diary:

> To me she [Charlotte] seemed a pleasant, well-dressed, well-intentioned woman. Now she turns out to be an 'original' with considerable personal charm and certain volcanic tendencies.... In a few days she and Bernard Shaw were constant companions.... To all seeming, she is in love with the brilliant Philanderer and he is taken in his cold way with her.

Occupied with work, and concerned that he would be accused of being a fortune-hunter, GBS turned down her proposals in July 1897, although their friendship continued, with Charlotte acting as his secretary when not travelling. By May 1898 Shaw had a large abscess on his left foot which required an operation. In a letter to Beatrice Webb he wrote:

> It was planned I must go away to the country the moment I could be moved, and that someone must seriously take in hand the job of looking after me. Equally plain, of course, that Charlotte was the inevitable and predestined agent, appointed by Destiny. To have her do this in any other character than that of my wife would (in the absence of your chaperonage) have involved our whole circle and its interests in a scandal. I found that my objection to my own marriage had ceased with any objection to my own death.

Shaw had recently found success with an American production of *The Devil's Disciple*: 'It did not make me as rich as my wife; but it placed me beyond all suspicion of being a fortune hunter or a parasite.'

On the afternoon of 1 June 1898 they married, with Shaw sending an unsigned report of the occasion to *The Star*: 'As a lady and gentleman were out driving in Henrietta St., Covent Garden yesterday, a heavy shower drove them to take shelter in the office of the Superintendent Registrar there, and in the confusion of the moment he married them.'

Their first year of married life was dominated by Shaw's various periods of convalescence: while coming downstairs on crutches on honeymoon, he fell and broke his left arm. Just over a year later, in October 1899, Beatrice Webb wrote in her diary: 'The Shaws have taken up residence in Charlotte's attractive flat over the School of Economics (Adelphi Terrace).... Charlotte and Shaw have settled down into the most devoted married couple, she gentle and refined, with happiness added thereto, and he showing no sign of breaking loose from her dominion.... It is interesting to watch his fitful struggles.' As for Charlotte, now over 40, her fears of maternity were disappearing, and 'there was never any question of breeding'.

'She is just like the portrait Sartorio made in Italy when she was in her first youth'

'A Respectable Married Man'

With new-found order in his private life, Shaw had time to devote himself to his work, when not being taken unwillingly on holidays by Charlotte. The years up to the First World War were among Shaw's most productive and creative, when he wrote some of his best known works, including *Caesar and Cleopatra, Man and Superman, Major Barbara, Androcles and the Lion* and *Pygmalion*. Shaw became fashionable: the Prime Minister came to the first night of *Major Barbara* in 1905, and Edward VII laughed so much during *John Bull's Other Island* that he broke his chair. Shaw's reputation was made.

Shaw's love-hate relationship with the GBS self-publicity machine continued: 'I always suffer torments of remorse when the degrading exhibition is over. However, the thing had to be done; and there was no doing it by halves.' Images of Shaw became widespread and continued to multiply for the remainder of his life. In 1906 Shaw wrote, 'My wife insists on dragging me to Paris for 12 days at Easter so that Rodin may make a bust of me!!!!!' Charlotte often encouraged him to sit as a way of preventing him from working. Over the next 30 years Shaw sat for many of the leading artists of the time. Prince Troubetzkoy, Sigismund de Strobl, Jacob Epstein, Augustus John, Dame Laura Knight and Yousuf Karsh were among the more famous, although Charlotte declared that if the Epstein bust came into their house, she would walk out of it.

The Nobel Prize for Literature was awarded to Shaw in 1926. 'I wrote nothing in 1925 and that is probably why they gave it to me'(© Les Prix Nobel)

Robert Morley, Wendy Hiller, Bernard Shaw, Blanche Patch and Gabriel Pascal during the filming of *Major Barbara* (1941)

The First World War was a turning point for Shaw. Within a few years the social world he knew, criticised and satirised had been destroyed. His targets and audiences for reform had altered beyond recognition. In addition, Shaw had written a deeply unpopular leaflet entitled *Common Sense about the War*, which had led people to say that Shaw was unpatriotic, damaging his popularity. This period encouraged Shaw to write more 'heavyweight' works such as *Heartbreak House* (1919) and *Back to Methuselah* (1921), before turning to *St Joan* in 1923, which restored him to public favour.

In 1926 Shaw was given the Nobel Prize for Literature and wrote that 'I am in the very odor of sanctity after *St Joan*'. 'The Nobel Prize has been a hideous calamity for me.... It was really almost as bad as my 70th birthday.' Refusing the prize money on the grounds that he had sufficient money for his needs, he donated the £7,000 to assist in the creation of an Anglo-Swedish Literary Foundation.

Other accolades followed, including an Oscar for best screenplay for the 1938 film of *Pygmalion*, starring Wendy Hiller and Leslie Howard. His collaboration with the producer Gabriel Pascal was based on friendship: 'G.B.S. never met a human being who entertained him more', according to his secretary, Blanche Patch. Their friendship translated itself into films of *St Joan*, *Major Barbara* and *Caesar and Cleopatra*.

Shaw as 'Man and Superman'. The front door knocker was presented to him by his friend Rosie Banks Danecourt

The Oscar (©A.M.P.A.S.®) in the Museum Room is inscribed 'Academy first award to George Bernard Shaw for writing screen-play of *Pygmalion*', in 1938

A scene from the film version of *Caesar and Cleopatra* (1945), starring Stewart Granger, Vivien Leigh and Claude Rains

A Retreat from London

The entrance front. 'People bother me. I came here to hide away from them'

Examples of the postcards Shaw had pre-printed with stock replies in response to the huge postbag he received from around the world

Although the Shaws always kept a flat in London – first at Adelphi Terrace and later at Whitehall Court – Ayot St Lawrence was their main home. Henry and Clara Higgs came from the London flat to take up positions as Head Gardener and Cook-Housekeeper with an under-gardener, chauffeur and two maids to complete the household. Once accepted into the village, Bernard Shaw became a noted, but distant, figure in the community, providing prizes for village competitions, a photograph of himself for people to guess his weight, speaking to the Sunday school on why he was so ugly, and to the Women's Institute on how to argue properly. Most days he would saw and split up logs with Charlotte in the garden before walking around the village with his West Highland terrier, Kim, and a pair of secateurs to trim back stray twigs from overgrown paths, before returning in time for a drink of chocolate or milk at 4.30.

Edith Reeves remembers that the Shaws were very good neighbours, dropping grass cuttings over the fence as fodder for their animals, giving away cabbages and other vegetables, whilst insisting on buying local raspberries and cherries. Old bills show that they were also supportive of local shops, ordering Shaw's 'knicker' tweed suit and the chauffeur's livery and boiler suits from a Welwyn tailor and his supplies from the Welwyn chemists including Ribena, insect repellent, Steradent, hot-water bottles, rosehip or fig syrups, cinnamon lozenges and cold cream soap. Shaw also bought all his stamps from the Post Office in Ayot, telling Jisbella Lyth, the Post Mistress, that she could sell his signed requests for 2½d to autograph hunters. She was already selling them for three guineas.

Between answering letters with his pre-printed cards and writing his own books in his revolving 'Retreat' at the bottom of the garden, GBS also entertained his many guests, while trying not to give in to the many fans and journalists who gathered outside his gates. He used to say that if Shakespeare had been pestered as much and had given way, he would have written far fewer plays. Those guests who were admitted reflected the Shaws' wide circle of friends and interests: Vivien Leigh, Gabriel Pascal, Danny Kaye, Gene Tunney (World Heavyweight Boxing Champion, 1926–8, who said, 'It was wonderful to be with G.B.S., but Charlotte was a good half of it'), Lady Astor, Sidney and Beatrice Webb, Ivan Maisky, the Russian Ambassador, and T.E. Lawrence. The last became a frequent visitor and particular friend of Mrs Shaw, who often sent parcels of food to his spartan cottage at Clouds Hill in Dorset, and exchanged books and letters. Most Sundays, Apsley Cherry-Garrard (a member of Captain Scott's last expedition to the Antarctic and author of *The Worst Journey in the World*) and his wife walked across the fields from their house nearby for lunch.

Shaw would always dress for dinner, even if no visitors were expected, commenting that Ayot St Lawrence was 'a village where nobody dreams of dressing'. After dinner he would play the piano to his wife, who lay upstairs in bed. He would play Beethoven and Mozart, and sing excerpts from operas and Irish songs, walking outside to look at the stars before retiring to bed.

Shaw in his tin-miner's hat sawing up logs in the garden for exercise – something he couldn't do in London

The Last Decade

After the outbreak of the Second World War in 1939, the Shaws spent increasing amounts of time at Ayot St Lawrence to avoid the air raids over London, as Charlotte was becoming very ill with osteitis deformans, which left her hunchbacked and unable to walk. She died on 12 September 1943, aged 86. Surprising himself at his grief, Shaw explained, 'I lived with Charlotte for 40 years, and now realise there was so much about her I didn't know', and he was sometimes seen in tears by villagers out walking.

Alice Laden, who had nursed Charlotte through her last illness, came to Ayot St Lawrence on the retirement of the Higgses, and so began a new era at Shaw's Corner, with Mrs Laden, 'the Aberdonian Dragon', to cook Shaw's vegetarian meals and to discourage callers.

Within a few weeks of Charlotte's death, GBS had contacted the National Trust about Shaw's Corner, to enquire, 'Has such a trifle any use or interest for the National Trust?' James Lees-Milne came down to investigate. He was shown into the Drawing Room:

Shaw's Corner is a very ugly dark red brick villa, built in 1902.... The quality of the contents of the room on a par with that of the villa. Indifferent water colours of the Roman Campagna, trout pools etc in cheap gilt frames.... Presently the door opened and in came the great man. I was instantly struck by the snow-white head and beard, the blue eyes and the blue nose, with a small ripe spot over the left nostril ... I had not expected the strong Irish brogue. G.B.S. said he wished to impose no conditions on

the hand over, but he did not wish the house to become a dead museum. Hoped it would be a living shrine.

Later Shaw wrote to Lees-Milne, 'I shall transfer from London all the pictures and statuettes and busts that are there to titivate Shaw's Corner as a showplace.'

Shaw spent the remainder of his life here. One of his last works was a rhyming guide to the garden and village illustrated by his own photographs. When once asked if he was well, he replied, 'At my age, young man, you are either well or dead'.

At the beginning of September 1950, Mrs Laden's ginger cat Bunch died, and Mrs Laden took a holiday in Scotland. On Sunday, 10 September, while pruning a greengage tree in the garden, Shaw fell, fracturing his left thigh, and blew the whistle he always carried to call for help. He underwent an operation to reset his leg, but was discovered to be suffering from long-standing kidney and bladder troubles. On being asked how he was, he replied, 'Everyone asks me that, and it's so silly when all I want to do is die, but this damned vitality of mine won't let me.'

He returned back home to be faced with such large crowds of reporters that a screen was erected to protect his privacy. His bed was brought downstairs into the Dining Room and facing the window so that he could see the view over the main lawn in his garden. On sunny days he was wheeled outside in a bath-chair, but his energy and will to live were slipping away. Announcing 'I am going to die', he fell into a coma and died shortly before 5am on 2 November 1950.

'I am a very old man, and weary of everything. What's the good of trying to repair an ancient monument?'

Miss Blanche Patch ('Cross Patch'), Shaw's faithful secretary for 30 years

Portrait of the 'harmless Mephistopheles, or the grumpy wicked uncle with a heart of gold', by Yousuf Karsh

Tour of the House

The Exterior

The New Rectory was built in 1902, but was soon found to be too large for the income of the village rector. Although it is a modest house, it is a fascinating survival in its own right, as it has some interesting Edwardian features, as well as contemporary textiles, furniture and stained glass. Its importance lies in its unspoilt, homely appearance, but principally, of course, in the man who lived here for 46 years – George Bernard Shaw, widely recognised as one of the great figures of English literature.

The front of the house faces north. Many of the servants' or functional rooms are on this side of the house: the reception rooms and main bedrooms are on the south side. Period features on the exterior include the decorative use of rubbed brick around the windows and the stained glass. On the front door is a knocker presented to Shaw by his friend Rosie Banks Danecourt, showing GBS in a large hat with the inscription 'Man and Superman'.

The Entrance Hall

A collection of Shaw's famous hats is inside the front door. A maid recalled that he would wear the wool felt hats in summer and the straw hats in winter. He used the tin-miner's hat (worn with the peak at the back to protect the neck), when chopping wood in the garden, to the delight of local children. GBS converted an old hat belonging to his housekeeper for beekeeping by adding a black veil. Nearby are his gaiters, shoes and walking sticks, one of which was given to him by William

Morris, who designed the 'Peacock and Dragon' pattern of the door curtain. The Arts and Crafts connection continues with the Bechstein piano, which was designed in about 1890 by Walter Cave, Secretary of the Art Workers' Guild.

Above the piano hangs a view of Capri; the painting on its left in the red frame is *First Night in the Stalls* by Dame Laura Knight. The Shaws probably bought, or were given, many of the pictures in the house on their frequent travels. The painting above the Dining Room door is by George Russell, known for his depictions of traditional Irish rural life.

The basket chair was used daily by Shaw as he stopped to put on his shoes and gaiters before going out for his walk. The other two rush-seated chairs reflect the fashion at the turn of the century for this style, again influenced by Morris. There would often be a basket of pink azaleas on the stand by the fireplace, brought by Ivan Maisky, the Russian Ambassador.

'The pianoforte is the most important of all musical instruments: its invention was to music what printing was to poetry'

First Night in the Stalls, by Dame Laura Knight (Entrance Hall)

The north front of Shaw's Corner. 'Mr Shaw was a prisoner in his own house. He could not even poke his head out of the window without someone spotting it' (Mrs Laden)

Shaw's Bechstein piano and collection of hats in the Entrance Hall

Rodin's bust of Shaw in the Drawing Room. 'Shaw as a model surpasses description. He has the power of getting his whole self into his bust which will have to represent the whole Shaw that Rodin has before him' (Rainer Maria Rilke, Rodin's secretary)

The collection of tools in the Study reveals Shaw's love of gadgets

The Study (*illustrated on back cover*)

The Study was Shaw's workroom, facing east and flooded with sunlight in the mornings. The books he needed for reference are close to hand, and the walls are hung with pictures of his friends, including Sidney Webb, Gene Tunney, Lady Gregory, W.B. Yeats and James Barrie. Not all these are original, and on close inspection, you will find that some were merely cut from newspapers, sandwiched between glass, and taped in the popular 'passe-partout' style of the day. To the left of the window hangs a portrait of William Morris. Over the reading bureau is a print by Aubrey Beardsley which was used as a controversial poster for the production of 'Arms And the Man' at the Avenue Theatre, London in 1894. On the left of the doorway is a portrait of Philip Wicksteed, an economist who convinced Shaw to turn his back on the Marxist theory of class war and to concentrate on the conflict between those who earned money ('producers') and the privileged unemployed who lived off rents.

The main desk was where Shaw wrote, and cut and pasted drafts of his texts, littering the floor with scraps of paper. The smaller 'secrytype' mahogany-finished desk was bought in 1932 for £6 18s 6d for Blanche Patch, his secretary for 30 years. The books on the shelves range from a collection of Dickens, Morris's complete works, and Shaw's copies of his own plays, to books on yoga, history, gardening and the early Soviet Government. Mrs Laden, Shaw's Housekeeper from 1943 to 1950, was amused by his filing system, with one drawer labelled 'Keys and Contraptions' and equally sized drawers marked 'Ayot' and 'Russia'. An unusual photograph shows Lord Howard de Walden, William Archer, Barrie, Chesterton and Shaw dressed as cowboys, when acting in a never-completed film by Barrie.

The Drawing Room

Compared with the Study, the Drawing Room was very much Mrs Shaw's room, with the portrait painted of her by G.A. Sartorio in Rome in 1895 hanging over the mantelpiece. All of the Italian landscape paintings on the right-hand wall are also by Sartorio. A maid recalled serving tea with cress sandwiches and cakes in this room from a table formed by using the large metal tray now on top of the desk.

Although Shaw had been an art critic early in his career, he much preferred sculpture to paintings, often taking his collection outside and photographing them in the garden. In the bay window are three bronzes by Prince Paul Troubetzkoy of Rodin, Shaw and Troubetzkoy's sister-in-law. Troubetzkoy was a Russian-American sculptor popular among the theatrical set, who often met the Shaws on holiday in Italy. Rodin's bust of Shaw (1906) sits on the bookcase. Rodin's head of Balzac is also in this room. On the small stool is a marble of Shaw's hand by Sigismund de Strobl. Although the maids arranged flowers for the Drawing Room, Shaw once remarked that he liked flowers, but he liked children too, and saw no reason to cut off their heads and stick them in water.

The Drawing Room

The Dining Room

Both the Drawing Room and Dining Room have doors out on to the terrace, Shaw's 'Riviera', where he would sit with friends enjoying the view. Shaw spent much time in this room, taking two or three hours over his midday meal, spreading out his letters over the table, and deciding which ones he would reply to. Mrs Laden recalled that towards the end of his life 'he lived on soups, eggs, milk, honey, cheese, fruit, cream and lemon juice'. His other staff remember him enjoying strawberries, yoghurt, jacket potatoes and often seeing him eating sweets, iced cake or spooning sugar from a bowl. In the evenings, after dinner he would sit listening to concerts on the radio, calling the BBC if he heard a wrong note.

The photographs on the chimneypiece represent Shaw's sympathies, and from left to right portray Gandhi, Dzerzhinsky (a Bolshevik and leader of the KGB), Lenin, Stalin, Granville-Barker (an actor and fellow playwright), 33 Synge Street (Shaw's birthplace), and Ibsen, whose photograph Shaw sent away to be framed just before his last illness. On his return from hospital, Shaw's bed was moved into this room and he died the day after the picture returned.

On the right-hand wall is Shaw's portrait by Augustus John, and framed scrolls recording him as a freeman of Dublin and St Pancras. The many prints of Dublin around the room link GBS to his early life in Ireland. The painting of ducks is by Scott of the Antarctic's son Peter, whom Shaw knew from infancy and who later became famous as the founder of the Slimbridge Wetland Trust. The photograph by the garden door of Shaw as the 'Chucker Out' was taken outside on the terrace: Shaw saw himself as the 'Chucker Out' of outdated Victorian moralism and politics. The black papier-mâché trays were a present from T.E. Lawrence to Mrs Shaw.

After Shaw's death, his ashes were mixed on the sideboard with Charlotte's by the Public Trustee before being taken and scattered in the garden and around the revolving hut.

The Staircase

A set of enlarged Bewick prints lines the stairs, reflecting Shaw's interest in birds. Fantail pigeons were kept in the garden, and Shaw fed the birds on bread soaked in marmite soup, with which he began lunch; unsentimentally, he never waited to see them feed. The little hearts in the staircase are a common feature of 20th-century houses, made popular by the architect Voysey. This was the staircase for the Shaws and their guests; the servants had their own staircase near the kitchen.

GBS received the Freedom of the Borough of St Pancras in 1946, recognising his earlier role as a councillor in the area

Influences on Shaw, from Gandhi to Ibsen. The Dining Room mantelpiece

The Dining Room. The calendar stopped on 2 November, the day Shaw died

23

The Bathroom

The Shaws' first flat in Adelphi Terrace had neither bathroom nor hot running water, so the large bath at Shaw's Corner must have been a luxury. Shaw bathed himself daily until his last illness, except during the Second World War, when he bathed weekly to save water, whereas Mrs Shaw continued to use a hip-bath kept under her bed, and a commode, with jugs of hot water and slop pails carried up by her maid. Shaw was always concerned with his diet and weighed himself regularly: towards the end of his life his weight fell from eleven to nine stone: 'I am losing weight so fast that I shall presently have totally disappeared. I look when stripped like a native in a famine picture, an imperfectly concealed skeleton.'

Shaw's Bedroom

The layout of Shaw's bedroom remains as in his day, with a screen to protect against nocturnal draughts, as Shaw slept with his window open. The wardrobe and chest of drawers contain his clothes – his tweed suits, plus-fours, thick underwear and long woollen stockings, hand-knitted by devotees so that there was always a left and a right foot. By the window are volumes of Shakespeare and the Bible.

The Museum Room

Originally Mrs Shaw's bedroom, this now houses a collection of Shaw memorabilia. Above the fireplace is a framed plaster plaque of 'Schorr' (Shaw's phonetic alphabet spelling of his own name) made

for the closing titles of the 1945 film *Caesar and Cleopatra*. In the corner hangs a Waldo Lanchester puppet of Shaw made for the play *Shakes versus Shav*, which was performed at Malvern on 9 August 1949. On the walls are some of Shaw's pre-printed cards that were sent in reply to common requests for money, autographs and information on Shaw's views concerning vegetarianism, capital punishment and temperance. Shaw's 1898 Velotrab DRP French exercise bike probably gave Mrs Shaw fewer anxious moments than his real bicycle, from which he took frequent tumbles. One display cabinet contains Shaw's personal effects, including pens and spectacles, and the Oscar for best screenplay, given for the film version of Pygmalion in 1938.

The Kitchen is reached by retracing your steps back down the stairs and through the Entrance Hall, passing the servants' stairs on the right.

Shakes versus Shav was a ten-minute puppet play written in 1949 'starring' Shakespeare and Shaw: 'Peace, jealous Bard: we are both mortal. For a moment suffer my glimmering light to shine'

Detail of a painting of a portable altar by the Belgian artist Léon de Smet that faced Shaw in bed

Converted to Jaeger's 'woollen clothing system', Shaw paid great attention to his clothes

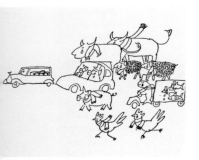

'My hearse will be followed not by mourning coaches but by herds of oxen, sheep, swine, flocks of poultry and a small travelling aquarium of live fish, all wearing white scarves in honour of the man who perished rather than eat his fellow creatures.' Cartoon by Tony Matthews

The Kitchen and Scullery

Mrs Higgs the Housekeeper prepared Shaw's vegetarian meals here and supervised the daily routine of housework. She was succeeded in 1943 by Mrs Laden. For the two maids, the day started at 6.30 with a cup of tea and a slice of bread and butter before going through to set the fireplaces and clean downstairs in complete silence. Mr and Mrs Higgs would have breakfast at 8, before the maids called the Shaws, taking Charlotte her tray upstairs and preparing her bath. During the morning the bedrooms would be cleaned and lunch prepared for 1, with tea at 4.30 and dinner at 8. An hors-d'oeuvres dish contained aspic jellies, chopped celery and tomato and diced beetroot. Potatoes and carrots were peeled evenly to be the same size, made into pyramids in a dish, and coated with melted butter and parsley. Shaw ate curry made with hard-boiled eggs, macaroni dipped in egg and bread-crumbs and fried, nut cutlets or macaroni cheese, but Mrs Shaw and their guests were not restricted to a vegetarian diet. Violet Liddle remembered caramel egg custards, junkets, fools, French pancakes baked on saucers and served with jam, and Queen's puddings made in the copper moulds kept on the dresser.

Shaw had been a vegetarian since January 1881, inspired by Shelley and lack of money. Unwilling to be a living grave for murdered animals, he also promoted the cause on world economic grounds. Privately, he would admit to being a vegetarian for humanitarian reasons, never killing a flea or a mouse vindictively or without remorse. Although drinking a little coffee, Shaw refused both tea and alcohol, saying that 'tea does more harm in the world than beer' and that alcohol 'enables Parliament to do things at eleven at night that no sane person would do at eleven in the morning'.

The staff ate the same food as the Shaws. Washing was sent out to a laundry. In the evenings the servants would sit in here, listening to the radio. The knife polisher in the alcove was a necessity before stainless steel became widespread. Many of the vegetables and fruit came from the garden, although a local Welwyn store provided lettuces, endives and grapes throughout the year. The large amount of post delivered each day was handed through the kitchen window by the postman.

VEGETARIAN DIET

Mr Shaw's correspondents are reminded that current vegetarianism does not mean living wholly on vegetables. Vegetarians eat cheese, butter, honey, eggs, and, on occasion, cod liver oil.

On this diet, without tasting fish, flesh, or fowl, Mr Shaw has reached the age of 92 (1948) in as good condition as his meat eating contemporaries. It is beyond question that persons who have never from their birth been fed otherwise than as vegetarians are at no disadvantage, mentally, physically, nor in duration of life, with their carnivorous fellow-citizens.

Nevertheless Mr Shaw is of opinion that his diet included an excess of protein. Until he was seventy he accumulated some poison that exploded every month or six weeks in a headache that blew it off and left him quite well after disabling him for a day. He tried every available treatment to get rid of the headaches: all quite unsuccessful. He now makes uncooked vegetables, chopped or grated, and their juices, with fruit, the staple of his diet, and finds it markedly better than the old high protein diet of beans, lentils and macaroni.

His objection to carnivorous diet is partly aesthetic, partly hygienic, mainly as involving an unnecessary waste of the labor of masses of mankind in the nurture and slaughter of cattle, poultry, and fish for human food.

He has no objection to the slaughter of animals as such. He knows that if we do not kill animals they will kill us. Squirrels, foxes, rabbits, tigers, cobras, locusts, white ants, rats, mosquitoes, fleas, and deer must be continually slain even to extermination by vegetarians as ruthlessly as by meat eaters. But he urges humane killing and does not enjoy it as a sport

Ayot Saint Lawrence,
Welwyn, Herts.

One of Shaw's pre-printed postcards prescribing his views on vegetarianism and his objections to eating meat

The Kitchen, which was ruled first by Mrs Higgs, then by Mrs Laden

The Garden

Shaw's 'masterful girl soldier' statue of St Joan in the garden

(*Right*) 'In shattering sunlight here's the shelter where I write dramas helter skelter' (Shaw's *Rhyming Picture Guide to Ayot St Lawrence*)

Extended in 1920, when Shaw bought extra land from his friend Apsley Cherry-Garrard, the garden is 1.4 hectares (3½ acres) in total. He took little direct interest in what was grown, leaving many decisions to his Head Gardener – first Mr Higgs, later Fred Drury. Outside the back door is the Pump House, originally operated by a manual pump, but later enlarged to contain an electric pump powered by the Engine or Accumulator House, which was built in 1930.

The lamb and lurcher figures on the terrace are by Troubetzkoy. Photographs show Shaw standing by the *Magnolia grandiflora* on the south side of the house. The garden was principally a place for relaxation and exercise, with an area set aside for the Shaws to chop wood. Drury and Higgs remembered the Shaws walking round the garden, deep in conversation. 'They used to put stones in a heap in a certain spot to mark every mile. They had a special route round the garden which was just about a mile, and they put one stone down every time they passed it…. They used to take them off the window sill on the way back, one by one.'

At the bottom of the garden is Shaw's revolving hut, which he would visit daily until the last year of his life in all weathers, as it was connected by electricity so that GBS could use an electric heater. The hut gave him a place of peace and quiet to retreat, and if visitors called, his Housekeeper could truthfully tell them that he was 'out'. He could turn the hut to improve the light or to change the view. He used to collect acorns, parcelled up in seven-pound bags, from the tree behind his hut to send to Sidney Webb to plant on his estate.

Shaw was particularly fond of the statue of St Joan in the Dell, which was made by his neighbour Clare Winsten, as he felt that this was how she should be portrayed: as a girl in peasant clothing, rather than as a soldier in armour.

The garage was built in 1922 to a design by the Garden City architect Barry Parker. At one time it housed three cars, including a Lanchester Ten and a chocolate-coloured 20 hp 'Silver Wraith' Rolls Royce. Fred Day, the chauffeur for 31 years, used to sit with Shaw while he was driving, 'fully occupied trying to keep him out of trouble'. GBS admitted, 'Putting my foot on the accelerator instead of the brake is becoming my favourite mistake'. Day was also asked to transport luggage, while the Shaws often preferred to travel by train.

Although the garden was turfed over after Shaw's death, the layout of the beds has now been restored using historical photographs and anecdotal evidence.

'He was very fond of his garden – used to walk around it a lot. It gave him the exercise without the need for going outside his gates' (Drury)

'He used to go down to his little wood hut to work regularly every day till his last year or so – where he went when it was fine, or when he was in the mood' (Drury)

A Living Shrine

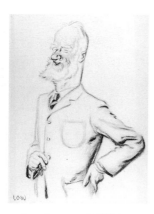

A caricature of GBS by David Low from the *New Statesman*, 1926

Mrs Laden opening Shaw's Corner to the public in 1951

Shaw's will provoked much confusion. His original intention to leave his royalties to sponsor a new phonetic alphabet found little support, and he left no money to endow Shaw's Corner, believing that the fees from visitors would fund its upkeep. After the alphabet scheme had been allocated a maximum of £8,300, annuities were given to the servants. His copyright income was then divided between the National Gallery of Ireland (which had given 'the only real education I ever got as a boy in Eire'), the Royal Academy of Dramatic Art, and the British Museum. Six weeks after Shaw's death in 1950, James Lees-Milne returned to Shaw's Corner with Harold Nicolson and Jack Rathbone, the Secretary of the National Trust. The Shaws' white ashes remained around the hut, rose bed and garden paths. The house was opened to the public by Edith Evans on 17 March 1951, with Mrs Laden as its first Custodian. She stayed a year:

> I almost felt that I was seeing his ghost at times, I couldn't get over the feeling that he would suddenly walk through the door or ask me for something through the hatch opening onto my kitchen.... We had a thousand cars coming through the village on busy Saturdays and Sundays the first summer the house was open to the public.

In 1951 Shaw's Corner was so popular that the police urged the National Trust to convert the large vegetable patch by the garage into a car-park.

Famous now mainly for his plays, in his lifetime Shaw's many interests appealed to a wide audience. He was playwright, music critic, keen advocator of vegetarianism, supporter of the women's movement, and tireless champion of socialist policies, with views on anything and everything from education, vaccination, Ireland and religion, to physical fitness, hygiene, war and marriage. He was determined to make people think and to question accepted opinion in an age of timidity: 'Mark Twain and I are in very much the same position. We have to put things in such a way as to make people, who would otherwise hang us, believe that we are joking.'

(*Above*) These framed mementoes hang in the Study

The back lawn today is often used as a stage for performances of Shaw's works